JAN 2018

STEM
ON THE BATTLEFIELD

DIRTY BOMBS AND SHELL SHOCK
BIOLOGY GOES TO WAR

LEON GRAY

Lerner Publications ◆ Minneapolis

Lerner Publications Company
A division of Lerner Publishing Group, Inc.
241 First Avenue North
Minneapolis, MN 55401 USA

For reading levels and more information, look up this title at www.lernerbooks.com.

Main body text set in Verdana Regular 11/16.5.
Typeface provided by Microsoft.

Picture Credits:

Front Cover © NEstudio/Shutterstock.
Interior: Department of Defense, 1; Robert Hunt Library, 4; Department of Defense, 5; Kamira/Shutterstock, 6; Robert Hunt Library, 7; Library of Congress, 8; Department of Defense, 9; Louvre Museum Paris, 10, 11; Robert Hunt Library, 12tr; Interfoto/Alamy, 12br; Department of Defense, 13; Thomastock, 14, 15bc; Library of Congress, 15cr; Robert Hunt Library, 16; Department of Defense, 17; Robert Hunt Library, 18; Library of Congress, 19tl; Everett Historical/Shutterstock, 19cr; Robert Hunt Library, 20; National Archives, 21; Bettmann/Getty Images, 22; Library of Congress, 23; Robert Hunt Library, 24, 25t; National Library of Medicine, 25cr; Robert Hunt Library, 26, 27tr; Interfoto/Alamy, 27bl; National Archives, 28; Library of Congress, 29; Wellcome Library, 30, 31tr; National Archives, 31br; National Library of Medicine, 32; Department of Defense, 33; Robert Hunt Library, 34; St John's College Cambridge, 35tr; Photographee.eu/ Shutterstock, 35br; Robert Hunt Library, 36, 37tr; science photo/Shutterstock, 37br; Wellcome Library, 38tc; National Archives, 38br; Department of Defense, 39; Photo Researchers/Mary Evans Picture Library, 40; Department of Defense, 41; Steve Shoup/Shutterstock, 42, Nestudio, 43.

Brown Bear Books has made every attempt to contact the copyright holder.
If you have any information please contact licensing@brownbearbooks.co.uk

Library of Congress Cataloging-in-Publication Data

Names: Gray, Leon, 1974– author.
Title: Dirty bombs and shell shock : biology goes to war / Leon Gray.
Other titles: Biology goes to war
Description: Minneapolis : Lerner Publications, [2018] | Series: STEM on the battlefield | Includes bibliographical references and index. | Audience: Grades 4–6. | Audience: Ages 9–12.
Identifiers: LCCN 2016059604 (print) | LCCN 2017000140 (ebook) | ISBN 9781512439281 (lb : alk. paper) | ISBN 9781512449501 (eb pdf)
Subjects: LCSH: Medicine, Military—Juvenile literature. | Biological warfare—Juvenile literature.
Classification: LCC UB369 .G73 2018 (print) | LCC UB369 (ebook) | DDC 355.001/57—dc23

LC record available at https://lccn.loc.gov/2016059604

Manufactured in the United States of America
1-42141-25414-4/26/2017

CONTENTS

BIOLOGY AT WAR

In 1914, Great Britain entered World War I (1914–1918). Within months, the British Army recruited thousands of men. When military doctors examined the recruits, they found that many suffered from poor health and sickness caused by a poor diet. The men were not fit enough to march long distances while carrying their packs. The doctors used their knowledge of **nutrition** to feed the recruits well. They made the men exercise to improve their physical fitness. Within a few months, the soldiers were strong and fit enough to handle the demands of serving on the front line, where they often had to march many miles carrying all their gear.

Two men applying to join the British Army in World War I are examined by military doctors in London.

LIFE SCIENCE

Biology is the branch of science concerned with living things. It includes medicine, veterinary care, nutrition, and mental health. Understanding biology has played a huge part in warfare. It has helped advance an understanding of nutrition, the science of food. It has helped doctors to find better ways to treat those who have been injured. Biologists have also used their understanding of **germs** and disease to develop powerful weapons that are designed to make people sick.

*Members of the US Army Chemical Corps practice evacuating a **casualty**. They wear gas masks, gloves, and hoods to protect them from a chemical attack.*

MEDICAL ADVANCES

Warfare has caused huge loss of life. However, it has also led to great advances in the sciences of biology and medicine. These advances include the discovery that germs cause disease and the invention of new methods of food preservation. Such innovations have helped military doctors and have also improved world health.

ANIMALS AT WAR

Animals have been used in warfare for thousands of years, both to carry or pull loads and for fighting. Armies that used animals learned how to keep animals strong and healthy.

One of the first animals used in warfare was the horse. Over four thousand years ago, warriors in Mesopotamia hitched horses to open vehicles called chariots and charged toward the enemy. One warrior used reins to steer the horses while others used bows to fire arrows from the platform at the back of the vehicle.

An Assyrian king drives a chariot into battle. The open platform allowed up to four warriors to ride together.

MOUNTED WARFARE

From around the eighth century CE, mounted warriors called knights dominated battlefields in Europe. Knights wore heavy armor, so their warhorses had to be very strong. Squires traveled with the knights to look after the horses and make sure they were given enough food. It was also essential for horses to be shoed, to protect their feet.

In the thirteenth century, the Mongols of central Asia built an empire using mounted archers to defeat enemy armies. Mongolian horses were stocky and had great **stamina**. The archers could advance deep into enemy territory.

SCIENCE FILE

Hannibal's Elephants

Elephants have a long history in warfare. Indian armies used elephants as early as the fourth century BCE. Hannibal was a military leader from the ancient North African city of Carthage on the Mediterranean Sea. When Carthage fought the ancient Romans, Hannibal led an army accompanied by elephants across the Alps mountains into Italy. He used the elephants in battle to defeat the Romans (218–201 BCE).

This painting shows Hannibal riding on an elephant. In battle, elephants were used to charge at enemy soldiers, sending them fleeing.

Horses pull gun carriages for a Union artillery battery during the Civil War. Five horses died in the war for every soldier who died.

HORSES IN LATER WARS

Horses were still used in warfare in the nineteenth and early twentieth centuries. In the US Civil War (1861–1865), horses pulled supply wagons and heavy guns. Officers led their men from horseback, and Confederate commanders also used cavalry to gather information by riding horse patrols into enemy territory. To keep the animals healthy, each horse was fed about 26 pounds of food per day. Armies needed hundreds of wagons of feed for their horses.

In World War I, horses were cared for by the British Royal Army Veterinary Corps (RAVC) and the US Army Veterinary Corps. Veterinarians cared for horses and treated millions of injured animals. As recently as World War II (1939–1945),

Killer Bats

Some armies have tried to use animals as weapons, but they usually have little success. In World War II, US forces planned to attach small fire bombs to hibernating bats. The army aimed to release the bats from planes over Japan, so that when they landed, they would start fires. The plan was scrapped when thousands of bats burned down a US Army airfield during tests in 1943.

horses were still used to transport soldiers and weapons.
These days, horses are used for ceremonial parades.
Veterinarians look after their welfare and nutrition.

A SOLDIER'S BEST FRIEND

In modern times, the RAVC also looks after military dogs.
During World War I and II, dogs carried messages to and
from troops on the front lines. In wars in Afghanistan and
Iraq, dogs have been used to detect mines and improvised
explosive devices. They work in K9, or canine, teams.
Dogs have a far better sense of smell than humans. While
humans have six million receptors for smell in their noses,
dogs have up to 300 million scent receptors. Dogs use
their sense of smell to sniff out buried explosives so that
they can be made safe. The RAVC trains the dogs and
their handlers and cares for any dogs that are injured.

*A K9 team
works with British
soldiers in Iraq.
The dogs wear
goggles to protect
their eyes in case
of an explosion.*

HEALTH AND FITNESS

Soldiers require speed, stamina, and strength on the battlefield. Being fit could mean the difference between life and death.

In nearly all armies throughout history, soldiers have had to march long distances on foot. In the Greek city-state of Sparta in around the fifth century BCE, society was centered around producing warriors. Boys were taken from their families at age seven and trained for twenty-three years in a military barracks. The boys were encouraged to fight one another to keep them tough. Sparta and other Greek city-states also promoted military skills such as wrestling and javelin throwing. These activities became the basis of the first Olympic Games.

An ancient Greek plate shows an athlete preparing to throw a discus. Such sports were all based on the skills required by Greek warriors.

Roman soldiers, or legionaries, had to be able to march 20 Roman miles (18.2 miles, or 29.3 kilometers). Soldiers exercised every day, training with heavy wooden weapons to build up their strength. To keep them fit, recruits were made to run, swim, carry heavy loads, and do long jump and high jump.

The ancient Roman writer Vegetius noted that Roman armies had an advantage over their enemies because their soldiers were strong enough to march over long distances.

IMPORTANCE OF FITNESS

In the Middle Ages, knights trained by lifting rocks to keep themselves strong enough to swing heavy swords or wrestle with an enemy. Around 1420, Italian physicians wrote that it was important for people to stay fit for their overall health. By the late sixteenth century, new exercise programs had begun to appear throughout Europe.

In the eighteenth century, Europe experienced a growth in **nationalism**. One result of this pride people had in their countries was a desire for a healthy population that was fit enough to serve in the army if necessary. In 1774 a gymnasium school opened in Germany to produce young men who could serve as soldiers. In the nineteenth century, Friedrich Jahn helped develop physical education as a subject. Other countries opened their own gymnasium schools. In the late nineteenth century, however, many people lived in poverty. Their diets were

THE BRAINS

Friedrich Jahn

(1778-1852) was a German educator who encouraged the development of gymnastics in Germany to prepare young men for military service. Jahn encouraged people to use equipment such as the rings and the parallel bars at open-air gymnasiums. He is sometimes called the father of gymnastics. Jahn's ideas spread widely in Europe in the nineteenth century.

Young Germans perform gymnastics at one of Friedrich Jahn's open-air gymnasiums, or Turnvereins.

poor, so they were physically weak. Their poor health also meant they suffered from diseases such as **rickets**. This proved a problem when countries tried to recruit armies at the start of World War I. New soldiers were too weak to perform well in battle. But by World War II, doctors studying nutrition reported that after serving time in the military, men were generally healthier than they had been as civilians due to better diets.

MODERN TESTS

Most modern armies set physical requirements that a recruit must pass to be admitted. Doctors test soldiers for strength and endurance. They also test cardiovascular fitness, which is the ability of the heart, lungs, and blood cells to provide oxygen-rich blood to the muscles.

SCIENCE FILE

Annual Test

Every year, US Army soldiers must pass a fitness test. They have to do two minutes of push-ups, two minutes of sit-ups, and a 2-mile (3.2-km) run. Female soldiers aged 17–21 must do at least 19 push-ups and 53 sit-ups, and must complete the run in less than 18 minutes, 54 seconds. Male soldiers aged 17–21 must complete at least 42 push-ups and 53 sit-ups, and complete the run in less than 16 minutes, 54 seconds.

US soldiers perform sit-ups. Modern soldiers can lose their jobs if they fail to achieve the required fitness levels.

NUTRITION

Military service is physically tough, so soldiers need to be in good health. Military doctors have figured out ways to make sure military personnel get the right food.

In wartime, military personnel are often on the move, so they need extra food to give them energy. Carbohydrates, from foods such as bread and pasta, provide energy. Fats, such as oils or cheese, also provide energy and help keep the body warm. Protein from meat or fish helps the body to repair damaged cells and can also develop muscle strength. Good nutrition helps soldiers to cope with stress by keeping the brain physically healthy. It also helps any physical wounds to heal more quickly.

In the late eighteenth century, the British Navy ordered its ships to carry supplies of citrus fruit, which contains vitamin C.

SCURVY

In the eighteenth century, many naval sailors suffered from scurvy. The disease causes fatigue and joint pain, and it can be fatal. More sailors died from scurvy than in combat. At sea, sailors lived on dried or salted food, which was easier to

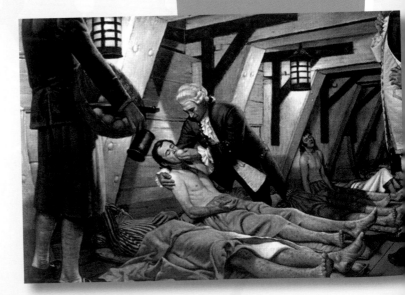

store on voyages. But the British physician James Lind carried out the first ever **clinical trial** in 1747. Sailors had noticed that fresh food helped reduce scurvy. Lind found that the best way to prevent scurvy was by giving sailors foods containing vitamin C, such as citrus fruit. Scurvy quickly disappeared.

PRESERVING FOOD

The need to feed sailors on long voyages or soldiers on long campaigns also encouraged scientists to look for better ways to preserve food. In 1795, the French military commander Napoleon Bonaparte offered a reward for anyone who could invent a new way to preserve food.

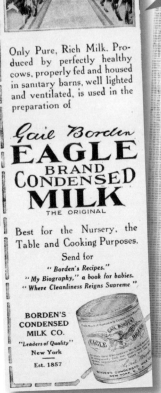

After the Civil War, condensed milk remained a popular form of canned food in many countries.

Only Pure, Rich Milk. Produced by perfectly healthy cows, properly fed and housed in sanitary barns, well lighted and ventilated, is used in the preparation of

Gail Borden
EAGLE
BRAND
CONDENSED
MILK
THE ORIGINAL

Best for the Nursery, the Table and Cooking Purposes.

Send for
"Borden's Recipes."
"My Biography," a book for babies.
"Where Cleanliness Reigns Supreme"

BORDEN'S
CONDENSED
MILK CO.
"Leaders of Quality"
New York
Est. 1857

THE BRAINS

Gail Borden

(1801–1874) was a US candy manufacturer. In the mid-1800s, he figured out a way to preserve fresh milk by making a sugary, syrupy mixture called condensed milk. It tasted good and stayed fresh in airtight tins. It gave soldiers the same nutrients as fresh milk, including fats and the mineral calcium, which keeps bones strong. In 1861, the Union Army placed a huge order for condensed milk to supply soldiers in the Civil War.

The chef Nicolas Appert experimented with ways to preserve food, and in 1810 he won Napoleon's reward by sealing food in airtight glass jars to keep it fresh. Appert's invention kept French soldiers fed and healthy during the Napoleonic Wars (1803–1815). A similar method of preserving food in tin cans appeared a few years later. Canned food was important in feeding troops in the US Civil War and in World War I.

CONTROLLING THE DIET

During World War I and II, military doctors figured out balanced diets to make sure that soldiers ate healthfully. The food had to be cheap, easy to prepare, and nutritious.

The improved understanding of nutrition also helped civilians. Food was in short supply, so governments handed out food in a system called rationing. Rationing made sure that everyone got a balanced diet. Although many people ate less during the wars, their health improved.

MILITARY NUTRITION

In the modern armed forces, nutrition is highly precise. Field kitchens provide food to those on the front line. Chefs design menus to give soldiers the nutrients they need to keep active and stay healthy. In combat, soldiers carry ration packs. These provide the energy required to sustain them in battle.

Preserved Rations

In combat, soldiers carry preserved food. The US military combat ration is called the Meal, Ready-to-Eat, or MRE. Each MRE provides about 1,200 calories to keep up a soldier's energy. Soldiers need at least 3,000 calories a day. MREs come in many options. They include a main dish such as pasta, meatballs, or chicken, a side such as vegetables, and a dessert or snack such as an energy bar. Some foods have extra minerals added. The MRE also includes a powdered drink such as tea or coffee, a dairy shake, or a fruit drink.

British soldiers eat supplies from 12-hour ration packs, which include a sandwich and beef jerky.

DISEASE AND SANITATION

Throughout history, more soldiers have been killed by disease than by the enemy. This only began to change in the late nineteenth century.

The main causes of disease among soldiers were usually crowded living conditions and a lack of **sanitation**. In an army camp, infectious diseases could easily spread through contact. Bathroom facilities were often open ditches at the edges of camp. There were inadequate washing facilities, so men could become infested with **lice**. They also developed skin **infections** from constantly wearing dirty, damp clothes and having few chances to change clothes or to bathe.

In crowded conditions like this military camp in the eighteenth century, soldiers lived close together. If one man became sick, he would infect many others.

Civil War soldiers wash in a pond. It was important to find fresh water to bathe in, as dirty water could cause diseases.

ROLE OF SANITATION

Until the late nineteenth century, people did not really know how disease spread. However, by the time of the US Civil War, doctors had come to understand the importance of good sanitation to prevent disease. In 1861, the US Sanitary Commission and the US Christian Commission encouraged soldiers to bathe frequently in fast-running water. They also raised money to pay for tents, blankets, and clothing, as well as medicines, to improve the general welfare and medical care of Union soldiers.

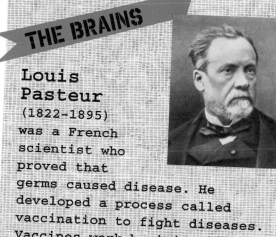

THE BRAINS

Louis Pasteur
(1822–1895) was a French scientist who proved that germs caused disease. He developed a process called vaccination to fight diseases. Vaccines work by injecting people with a weak form of a germ. This helps the body to develop ways to fight off the germ. Vaccination helped armies keep soldiers healthy.

IN THE TRENCHES

By World War I, scientists understood far more about disease. Louis Pasteur had proved that disease was spread by germs. In World War I, soldiers lived in dirty, cramped trenches, but they were regularly moved out of the trenches so they could rest and get back their strength. Many soldiers, however, suffered from a condition called trench foot. When the feet are damp for a long time, they swell up, restricting the flow of blood to the feet. The skin on the feet turns blue and begins to rot. Army doctors learned that the best way to prevent trench foot was for soldiers to keep their feet clean and dry. They gave soldiers clean socks and better boots. They asked soldiers to examine one another's feet for signs of infection, so that it could be treated early.

*British soldiers carry comrades suffering from trench foot. A badly affected foot might need to be **amputated** to stop infection from spreading.*

FIGHTING INFECTION

Soldiers wounded by gunfire or explosions on the battlefield are at high risk of infection. If the skin is broken, germs can quickly spread inside open wounds. During World War II, doctors began to use new drugs called **antibiotics** to prevent wounds from becoming infected. The military also improved the process of moving casualties from the battlefield to a clean hospital as quickly as possible. That gave infection less time to take hold.

SCIENCE FILE

Malaria

In the South Pacific in World War II, US forces suffered eight times more casualties from malaria than from enemy action. Malaria is passed into the blood by a mosquito bite. US authorities sprayed areas around camps with the insecticide DDT to kill mosquitos. They issued anti-malaria drugs to soldiers. Many men refused to take the drugs, however, because of false rumors that they caused problems with having children.

FIELD MEDICINE

In war, soldiers often suffer serious injuries. Casualties need to be treated on the battlefield. Medical care in a combat zone is called field medicine.

Ambroise Paré was a French military surgeon in the sixteenth century. At the time, there was little medical care available for wounded soldiers on the battlefield, but Paré believed that it was possible to help them survive. He bandaged wounds to stop soldiers from bleeding to death.

Ambroise Paré bandages a wounded soldier in a barn near the battlefield during fighting in France in the sixteenth century.

MORE ADVANCES

The first major development in field medicine came during the Napoleonic Wars (1803–1815), when the French were fighting Britain, Russia, and their allies. The French surgeon Dominique Jean Larrey used carriages to take wounded soldiers to the hospital. Larrey also introduced triage, in which a doctor or nurse decides in what order to treat casualties. They treated urgent cases first, but only if it was likely that a patient could be saved.

Anesthesia

Until the 1850s, patients were conscious during operations. In the Crimean War (1853–1856), the Russian surgeon Nikolay Pirogov used anesthesia to make patients unconscious during operations.
By the time of the Civil War, anesthesia was common. Patients inhaled the fumes of a chemical to knock them out. In modern times, most anesthetics are injected straight into the bloodstream.

An assistant in a US Civil War field hospital holds a cloth soaked in the chemical chloroform over a patient's face to anesthetize him while a surgeon operates on his leg.

THE WORLD WARS

During World War I, amputation methods improved and field hospitals were kept cleaner, so it was less likely that operations such as amputation would lead to infection. There were also advances in **blood transfusion**, which involves replacing blood lost from wounds or surgery with blood from someone else. Canadian and British doctors carried out the first blood transfusions in field hospitals, and built up the army's supplies of blood.

In the Spanish Civil War (1936–1939), the doctor Frederic Durán-Jordà set up a **blood bank** in Barcelona, where volunteers gave blood for soldiers. Durán-Jordà helped set up blood banks in Britain during World War II. The British Army Blood Supply Depot took more than 700,000 donations of blood during the war.

A casualty arrives at a hospital in World War I. Doctors will assess his priority for treatment based on his wounds.

US medics treat casualties outside a field hospital in France after the landings on D-day, June 6, 1944.

TCCC

Modern US armed forces have a system of field medicine called Tactical Combat Casualty Care (TCCC). Medics treat wounded men on the battlefield, even when under fire. They radio for stretcher bearers or a medical helicopter to evacuate the casualty. While the casualty waits for evacuation, medics continue to treat any serious injuries.

THE BRAINS

Charles R. Drew (1904–1950) was a US physician who studied blood transfusion. Blood has two parts: a liquid called plasma, and red blood cells. Drew tried putting only plasma into a patient during a transfusion. He found that the patient's body created its own red blood cells. In the 1930s, Drew set up blood banks in the United States. In World War II, Drew's blood banks made more blood available for injured soldiers.

MEDICAL TRANSPORTATION

Doctors know that the chances of a wounded soldier surviving are greatly increased by the speed with which he or she can be moved from the battlefield to a hospital.

An early record of medical evacuation comes from the late fifteenth century. The Spanish Army employed people to move casualties from the battlefield. The wounded men were carried on carts pulled by hand. Casualties had to wait for the fighting to stop before they were collected. By then, many soldiers were dead from their wounds.

Nineteenth-century ambulances were usually converted artillery wagons.

Medical transportation remained basic until the Napoleonic Wars. The French surgeon Dominique Jean Larrey set up the first army ambulance corps. Larrey realized that evacuation helped casualties survive their injuries. He adapted horse-drawn artillery wagons to create "flying ambulances." The wagons quickly moved casualties off the battlefield for medical help.

AIR EVACUATION

The airplane was invented in 1903. Less than twenty years later, the first air evacuation took place.

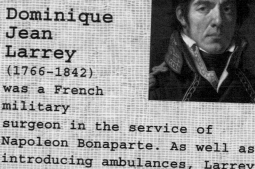

THE BRAINS

Dominique Jean Larrey (1766–1842) was a French military surgeon in the service of Napoleon Bonaparte. As well as introducing ambulances, Larrey performed some of the earliest field operations, including amputation. He also developed the system of triage, which sorted patients into the order in which they would be treated based on priority, regardless of their rank.

This photograph from the 1920s shows an ambulance plane operated by the US Army.

In 1917, during World War I, a British soldier was wounded in Turkey. The Royal Flying Corps flew him to the hospital in 45 minutes. Evacuation by land would have taken days. Records suggest that evacuating wounded soldiers by air could have cut the number of deaths caused by wounds from 60 percent to 10 percent.

During World War II, the US Army Air Corps set up medical air-evacuation squadrons. Aircraft carried doctors and nursing staff to provide medical care during a flight.

Medevac

Medical evacuation is often called medevac. It involves moving wounded soldiers from the battlefield as quickly as possible. Medevac usually involves evacuation by air-ambulance helicopters. Nurses provide emergency medical care during the flight to a field hospital. Medevac vehicles are unarmed and clearly marked. They take no part in combat. The enemy is supposed to let them travel freely.

A nurse checks patient details during a medevac flight on a C-47 Skytrain, a military transport aircraft acting as an air ambulance.

HELICOPTER POWER

After World War II, the US Air Force formed the Military Air Transport Service (MATS). During the Korean War (1950–1953), the MATS used helicopters to transport casualties to field hospitals for emergency treatment. The patients were later moved to hospital ships in the ocean close to the Korean coast. From there, airplanes flew them to permanent medical facilities in the United States.

Military aircraft are still used as air ambulances. The US military is testing the possibility of moving casualties with unmanned aerial vehicles (UAVs), or drones. These vehicles may be able to evacuate casualties more quickly and safely during battle.

HOSPITALS AND NURSING

War casualties in field hospitals or in larger military hospitals are looked after by nurses. Until the mid-nineteenth century, these nurses were usually untrained volunteers.

During the 1800s, nursing became more scientific. In the Crimean War (1853–1856), British nurse Florence Nightingale recruited trained nurses to look after wounded British soldiers in Turkey. Nightingale kept the wards clean, had the bedclothes changed frequently, and fed the soldiers well. The recovery rates increased dramatically.

Florence Nightingale made sure her hospital at Scutari, in Turkey, was light and airy. She even had a sewer moved because the fumes were affecting the patients.

CIVIL WAR

During the US Civil War, the former teacher Clara Barton looked after wounded Union soldiers. In August 1862, she persuaded Union authorities to allow her to work on the front line. She distributed medical supplies, cleaned field hospitals, and dressed soldiers' wounds. Barton treated casualties from many battles, from both the Union and Confederate sides. After the war, she was responsible for founding the American Red Cross in 1881, and later the National First Aid Society.

Florence Nightingale (1820–1910) became famous in the Crimean War. She worked in a hospital nursing wounded British soldiers. Nightingale prevented thousands of deaths by improving hygiene. After the war, she set up a nursing school in London. The school helped to improve training for all types of nurses.

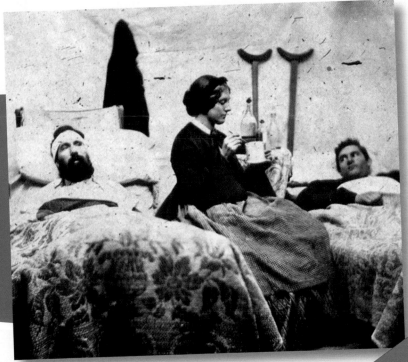

A volunteer nurse brings water to patients in a Union hospital during the Civil War. Nurses often had little experience apart from what they had learned caring for their families.

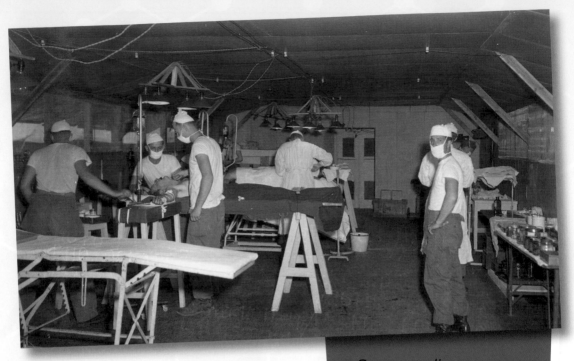

FIELD HOSPITALS

The US Army Nurse Corps (ANC) was set up in 1901. ANC nurses served in field hospitals in both world wars and in later conflicts such as the Vietnam War. Modern military nurses are service personnel recruited by each of the US armed forces.

Surgeons discuss treatments in a MASH in the Korean War. MASH doctors in Korea improved methods of triage and figured out better ways to store blood for transfusions.

Field hospitals are often made up of several large tents staffed by surgeons, doctors, and nurses. Field hospitals appeared at the end of World War II, when the US Army set up Mobile Army Surgical Hospitals (MASH). MASH units were widely used in the wars in Korea and Vietnam. The hospitals were close to the front line, so casualties could be treated as quickly as possible. That increased their chances of survival.

COMBAT SUPPORT

In 2006, the US military replaced MASH units with Combat Support Hospitals (CSH). These can be very large, with hundreds of beds and several operating rooms laid out in a complex of large tents. There are medical laboratories for blood tests and a **pharmacy** to supply medicines. CSHs also have equipment such as X-ray machines or scanners. CSHs are not as mobile as MASH units. Casualties receive care on the battlefield from forward-support teams before helicopters take them to the CSH.

Wounded soldiers in one of the tent wards of the 325th Combat Support Hospital. The CSH is delivered to a war zone in cargo containers, then assembled.

SCIENCE FILE

Prosthetics

Wounds caused by explosions in combat leave many soldiers needing amputations. In the past, many amputees were given basic prosthetic limbs. Modern limbs are more advanced. Some even have microprocessors that help the prosthetic move in the same way as natural limbs. Because of modern prosthetics, it is sometimes possible for amputees to return to active duty.

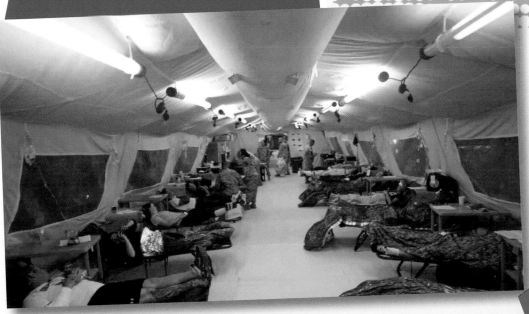

MENTAL HEALTH

In World War I, some soldiers suffered a mental-health condition called shell shock. It was caused by being constantly under fire.

Men with shell shock lost their courage and entered a daze. At the time, many doctors did not take shell shock seriously. They sent soldiers back to fight, even if the men were no better than before. Since then, experts have learned more about mental health. They know that the **trauma** of warfare puts great mental strain on soldiers.

Soldiers sometimes experience traumatic events. They might witness death and injury, or narrowly escape death themselves. These experiences can cause problems such as depression, anxiety, or substance abuse. Such symptoms are now seen as signs of post-traumatic stress disorder (PTSD).

A British World War I soldier stares into space. Some men who suffered from stress and were unable to fight were wrongly accused of cowardice.

People suffering from PTSD may suffer flashbacks and nightmares caused by their wartime experiences. They might suffer panic attacks and mood swings.

PSYCHIATRIC CARE

Doctors called **psychiatrists** treat mental-health disorders. They offer cognitive behavioral therapy (CBT). This program encourages soldiers to talk about their traumatic experiences. Psychiatrists also give counseling to the families of affected soldiers. That helps families to support the patient. With time and professional help, many sufferers are able to get relief from their symptoms, or even overcome them altogether.

THE BRAINS

W.H.R Rivers (1864–1922) was a British psychiatrist. During World War I, he came up with a new treatment for shell shock. Rivers encouraged soldiers to discuss their wartime experiences. Rivers found that this "talking cure" helped to reduce the soldiers' stress, so they could return to better mental health.

Modern treatment for PTSD includes sessions of CBT, when sufferers discuss their experiences with a trained psychiatrist.

PENICILLIN

The discovery of penicillin was a turning point in medicine. The new drug allowed doctors to treat and cure infectious diseases that had once been deadly.

Penicillin was one of the world's first antibiotics. These are drugs that kill the germs that cause disease. The germs spread by building cells inside the human body. Antibiotics destroy the germs' ability to create cells, so the disease cannot survive.

*Early battlefields had ideal conditions for **bacteria** to thrive. Bacteria infected soldiers' open wounds.*

The Scottish physician Alexander Fleming discovered penicillin by accident in 1928. Fleming returned from vacation and noticed mold growing in a **petri dish**. The dish contained bacteria that Fleming had been working on before his vacation. There were no bacteria in the area around the mold because something in the mold was killing them. This substance turned out to be penicillin.

THE NEXT STAGE

Ten years later, two researchers at Oxford University read about Fleming's discovery. They were the Australian Howard Florey and the German Ernst Chain. They realized that penicillin might be a useful medicine if they could figure out a way to produce it on a large scale. They set up a laboratory together to begin work.

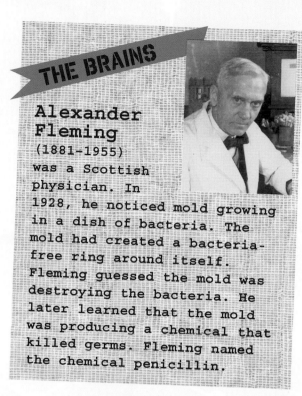

THE BRAINS

Alexander Fleming
(1881–1955) was a Scottish physician. In 1928, he noticed mold growing in a dish of bacteria. The mold had created a bacteria-free ring around itself. Fleming guessed the mold was destroying the bacteria. He later learned that the mold was producing a chemical that killed germs. Fleming named the chemical penicillin.

Fleming was growing bacteria when he noticed the effect of mold on the surrounding bacteria.

Ernst Chain

(1906–1979)
was a German
scientist who
moved to Britain
when the Germans began
persecuting Jews in 1933.
Chain worked with Howard
Florey to figure out the
chemical composition of
penicillin. On his own, he
learned to isolate the part of
penicillin that killed germs.

While Florey and Chain were working, World War II broke out in Europe. It was clear that many soldiers would die if their wounds became infected with bacteria. That made Florey and Chain's work more urgent. In 1941, they successfully used penicillin to cure a patient of a severe infection. Florey then worked in the United States with the neurosurgeon Hugh Cairns to figure out the most efficient way to use small doses of penicillin to treat war wounds.

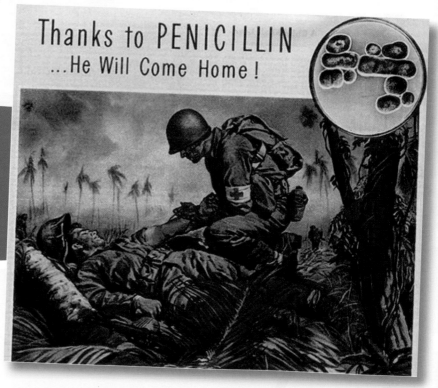

Thanks to PENICILLIN
...He Will Come Home!

This poster from World War II shows a US medic injecting penicillin into a wounded soldier on the battlefield.

PENICILLIN IN WORLD WAR II

Penicillin was soon delivered to Allied soldiers around the world. It gave them an advantage over their German and Japanese enemies, who did not have the medicine. The antibiotic saved the lives of many wounded soldiers. It prevented their wounds from becoming infected with diseases such as **gangrene**. Often limbs affected by gangrene needed to be amputated. Many operations took place in insanitary conditions, but penicillin also dramatically cut the number of infections contracted after surgery. Penicillin was also effective against a blood infection called septicemia, which can cause organ failure. For their contribution to medicine and the Allied cause in World War II, Alexander Fleming, Howard Florey, and Ernst Chain won the Nobel Prize in Physiology or Medicine in 1945.

Penicillin is still used in field medicine, although some bacteria have become resistant to antibiotics.

BIOLOGICAL WARFARE

Biological warfare describes the use of weapons that use germs to cause deadly diseases. Biological weapons are known as weapons of mass destruction (WMDs). Other WMDs include dirty bombs and nuclear weapons.

Biological weapons have existed for at least 2,500 years. In 590 BCE, ancient Greek soldiers extracted deadly chemicals from plants. They used the chemicals to poison the water supplies of their enemies. In the Middle Ages, Mongol warriors from Central Asia moved west. They conquered large areas. The Mongols used dead bodies as biological weapons. They gathered bodies of soldiers who had died of **bubonic plague** and used

Attackers fire the heads of soldiers who have died from plague into a town in the eleventh century.

catapults to fire the dead bodies over the walls of enemy castles or cities. The deadly plague soon spread and killed the people inside.

USING GERMS

Scientists in many countries started to develop biological weapons during the twentieth century. British scientists made weapons using germs called **anthrax** and **botulism**. These germs cause deadly diseases. Japanese scientists also produced biological weapons. During the Sino-Japanese War with China (1937–1945), Japanese pilots flew over the Chinese city of Ningbo. They dropped bombs containing fleas infected with bubonic plague.

US Army Chemical Corps

The Chemical Corps is part of the US Army. It deals with the threat of chemical, biological, radiological, or nuclear (CBRN) attack. The Chemical Corps originated in World War I as the Chemical Warfare Service (CWS). Its task was to combat the use of poison gas on the battlefield. The CWS was renamed the Chemical Corps at the end of World War II. These days it focuses mainly on dealing with incidents involving CBRN weapons.

Members of the US Army Chemical Warfare Corps carry out a military exercise wearing full protective clothing.

After World War II, US researchers experimented with using germs to cause diseases such as anthrax and tularemia (rabbit fever). The US Army Chemical Corps developed bombs that sprayed germs over wide areas. These weapons were never used in battle.

BIOTERRORISM

In 1975, many countries signed an agreement drawn up by the Biological and Toxin Weapons Convention. The agreement banned the manufacture and use of biological weapons. However, there is still a threat from terrorists who may have biological weapons that can spread disease. An attack using these weapons is called bioterrorism. The risks of bioterrorism are high because it is easier for terrorists to get biological materials than chemical or **radioactive** substances.

TERROR ATTACKS

Biological attacks are rare, but they have happened. In 1995, members of a religious cult released a poison gas in the Tokyo subway. The attack killed thirteen people. In 2001, terrorists mailed letters to government officials in Washington, DC. The envelopes contained anthrax. The poison killed five people and infected seventeen more. It is possible that similar attacks will take place in the future. Biologists will be at the heart of attempts to defeat future acts of bioterrorism.

The Chemical Corps wear special suits to protect them from an attack using chemicals or dirty bombs.

TIMELINE

590 BCE — Greek soldiers poison the water supplies of their enemies with deadly chemicals taken from plants.

218–201 BCE — Hannibal of Carthage marches elephants across the Alps before defeating the Roman Army.

1795 — The French military offers a prize for a new method of food preservation.

1810 — Nicolas Appert wins the prize for preserving food in airtight glass containers.

1861 — The Union Army places the first order for Gail Borden's condensed milk.

1901 — The US Army Nurse Corps is established.

1917 — The first medical air evacuation takes place in Turkey during World War I.

1928 — Alexander Fleming discovers penicillin.

1940 — Japan uses bubonic plague as a biological weapon in the Sino-Japanese War (1937–1945).

1942	Florey and Chain manufacture penicillin.
1943	Bats carrying small explosive devices cause a fire at a US Army airfield.
1945	Alexander Fleming, Howard Florey, and Ernst Chain win the Nobel Prize in Physiology or Medicine for their discovery and development of penicillin.
1975	Countries sign up to the Biological and Toxin Weapons Convention, outlawing the manufacture and use of biological weapons.
2001	An anthrax attack occurs in Washington, DC.
2006	Combat Support Hospitals replace Mobile Army Surgical Hospitals.
2016	The number of countries that have signed up to ban biological weapons rises to 165.

INDEX